MIDLOTHIAN PUBLIC LIBRARY

3 1614 00200 9133

W9-ANP-622

Exploring Infrastructure

DAMS AND LEVEES

Kevin Reilly

MIDLOTHIAN PUBLIC LIBRARY
KENTON AVENUE
445

Enslow Publishing
101 W. 23rd Street
Suite 240
New York, NY 10011
USA

enslow.com

JW
627.8 T
6 Re

For the victims of Hurricane Katrina, and for those working to ensure that the levees never fail New Orleans again

Published in 2020 by Enslow Publishing, LLC.
101 W. 23rd Street, Suite 240, New York, NY 10011

Copyright © 2020 by Enslow Publishing, LLC.

All rights reserved

No part of this book may be reproduced by any means without the written permission of the publisher.

Library of Congress Cataloging-in-Publication Data

Names: Reilly, Kevin, author.
Title: Dams and levees / Kevin Reilly.
Description: New York : Enslow Publishing, 2020. | Series: Exploring infrastructure | Audience: Grades 3 to 6. | Includes bibliographical references and index.
Identifiers: LCCN 2018016628| ISBN 9781978503342 (library bound) | ISBN 9781978505087 (pbk.)
Subjects: LCSH: Dams—Juvenile literature. | Levees—Juvenile literature. | CYAC: Dams. | Levees. | LCGFT: Instructional and educational works.
Classification: LCC TC541 .R45 2019 | DDC 627/.8—dc23
LC record available at https://lccn.loc.gov/2018016628

Printed in the United States of America

To Our Readers: We have done our best to make sure all website addresses in this book were active and appropriate when we went to press. However, the author and the publisher have no control over and assume no liability for the material available on those websites or on any websites they may link to. Any comments or suggestions can be sent by email to customerservice@enslow.com.

Photo Credits: Cover, p. 1 saiko3p/Shutterstock.com; cover, pp. 1, 3 (top) Panimoni/Shutterstock.com; p. 5 SGeneralov/Shutterstock.com; p. 6 The Asahi Shimbun/Getty Images; p. 9 Gerrit Bunt/Shutterstock.com; p. 10 Beckamrajeev/Wikimedia Commons/File:Grand Anicut kallanai.JPG/CC BY-SA 3.0; p. 13 Alinari Archives/Getty Images; p. 15 Adrian Ace Williams/Archive Photos/Getty Images; p. 17 Deni Williams/Shutterstock.com; p. 18 Somrerk Witthayanant/Shutterstock.com; p. 22 ESB Professional/Shutterstock.com; p. 25 William Taufic/Corbis/Getty Images; p. 26 Cultura Creative (RF)/Alamy Stock Photo; p. 29 pisaphotography/Shutterstock.com; pp. 30, 39 Bettmann/Getty Images; p. 34 Jeff Topping/Getty Images; p. 37 Stock Montage/Archive Photos/Getty Images; p. 41 Library of Congress/Corbis Historical/Getty Images; p. 42 Justin Sullivan/Getty Images.

CONTENTS

INTRODUCTION

Changing the Environment
to Make Life Easier

Beavers are some of the coolest animals in North America. At first, they might not remind you much of people. They have big flat tails and long buck teeth. But they are very similar to humans in one way. They change their environment to make life easier for themselves.

Most animal homes are pretty basic. Not the beaver's! Beavers build big, complicated homes called beaver dams. First, beavers find a nice spot along a stream or creek. Then they cut down trees with their sharp teeth. They build a long pile of sticks, rocks, and mud all the way across the water. They make sure to leave enough space to live on the inside of the dam. Then they build an underwater entrance. Finally, they pat down the outside with their tails. When it's finished, the beaver dam floods the outside area on one

A beaver dam. Beavers and humans both build dams to improve their quality of life.

of its sides. This helps the beavers hide from predators. It also lets them catch fish more easily. Beaver dams also improve the area for other animals that can't build such great houses on their own.

It might seem weird to think about, but humans build dams for very similar reasons! A dam is a barrier that stops the flow of water. People use dams to store water from rivers and lakes. That water can be used for drinking, irrigating crops, and getting around water- ways more easily. Also, machines can help us use the energy of the water that moves through dams. Energy that comes from moving water is called hydropower.

A new levee is built in Kesennuma, Japan, in 2017. Much of the area was destroyed by a tsunami in 2011.

Dams make it much easier for people to live in places that they normally couldn't. Let's think about Las Vegas, Nevada. The city is in the middle of the desert. But millions of people live there and there are many amazing hotels and casinos. This is possible because of a dam! Hoover Dam blocks the Colorado River and provides most of the city's drinking water and much of its electricity. We'll learn a lot more about the incredible Hoover Dam later on.

A Look at Levees

There is another structure that is a lot like a dam. It is called a levee. A levee is a very long wall or ridge that is used to keep water levels from getting too high. Levees are built next to rivers and lakes. They are used to keep low-lying areas from flooding. There are many levees in the Netherlands. This is because only half of the entire country is more than 3 feet (1 meter) above sea level! In a later chapter, we'll zoom in on the city of New Orleans in Louisiana and find out why its levees are so important.

Dams and levees are some of the most important structures that humans have ever built. Without them, some of the most wonderful cities and towns couldn't exist. Millions of people wouldn't be able to have electricity. Scientists and engineers are working very hard to make our dams and levees even better. We want to be sure that they give us clean electricity and water far into the future.

Let's learn more about dams and levees. And don't forget: the next time that you go hiking in the woods near a stream or creek, keep your eyes peeled for beaver dams!

Chapter 1

EARLY DAMS AND LEVEES

Dams and levees go all the way back to the very beginning of human history. Five thousand years ago, civilization as we know it began in Mesopotamia. This was an area between the Tigris and Euphrates Rivers in the Middle East. People in this area learned to use their natural environment and grow crops. This meant that they could stay in one place instead of moving around and hunting. They also built the first dams and levees. These structures shifted water from the two rivers into their fields. This helped the plants grow. This kind of farming is called irrigation.

Since they didn't have to spend all of their time hunting for food, the Mesopotamians were able to spend time on other things. They invented the earliest forms of written language, mathematics, astronomy, and many other key parts of human society. None of this would have been possible without dams and levees!

A view of the Euphrates River. The people of Mesopotamia built the first dams on the Tigris and Euphrates rivers.

The First Dams

Long ago, people built two kinds of dams: gravity dams and embankment dams. Embankment dams are the simplest. First, builders packed down huge amounts of earth in a big slope. By doing this, they could direct the flow of water. These dams would wear down rather quickly. They didn't last long. Gravity dams are a bit more complicated. People made a barrier out of a gigantic pile of rocks. It was so heavy that gravity wouldn't let the water break it apart. The Jawa Dam is the oldest known dam in the world. It was a gravity dam built in 3000 BCE.

The Kallanai Dam sits on the Cauvery River in India.
It is still in use after almost two thousand years.

One of the most impressive embankment dams built during this time was the Great Dam of Marib in Yemen. It is called an engineering wonder of the ancient world. It was first built around 1750 BCE. Builders piled up stones on opposite sides of the river. Then they filled in the middle with a huge triangle of packed earth. Over time, different tribes took control of the land. They added their own improvements to the Great Dam. It ended up being 46 feet (14 m) high. Once it was completed in 325 CE, it was able to irrigate 25,000 acres (10,117 hectares) of crops.

Ancient dams did not work as well as the ones we build today. The people who made them didn't have today's tools and technology. But they were an important first step.

Ancient Roman Builders Improve Dams and Levees

The next important group after the Mesopotamians was the ancient Romans. They were master builders. They greatly improved the way that dams and levees were built. They did not use rocks and earth to build their structures. Instead, they invented a strong material that we still use today: concrete! Their embankment and gravity dams were built out of solid concrete. This meant that they were much less likely to be damaged. They also moved water much more easily than earlier structures.

The Romans didn't have to spend all of their time and energy repairing broken dams. So they were able to experiment with more advanced shapes and sizes. Modern dams are built using much better technology. But most of the

The Kallanai Dam

The Kallanai Dam is the oldest dam on earth that is still in use today. It was built in the second century CE in India. The dam helped irrigate crops by moving water from the Kaveri River into nearby deltas. The British updated the dam in the 1800s in order to make water move through it better. Today, it irrigates over 1 million acres (404,685 ha) of land. It is still in very good condition.

designs we use today can be traced back to the inventions of this exciting time period.

One of the most common types of dams built by the Romans was the arch dam. Gravity dams were built straight across a river. Arch dams are slightly curved upstream. This design keeps the flowing water from putting too much pressure on the dam. This means that it's much less likely to burst during a flood. Arch dams also need fewer materials than other designs. This makes them less costly to build.

Ancient Romans also created the first buttress dams. On the upstream side, these dams can look just like gravity or arch dams. But on the downstream side, they are supported by a series of strong concrete pillars called buttresses. This feature helps prop up the dams against water pressure even better.

The last major type of dam that the ancient Romans invented was the bridge dam. You guessed it: these are dams that are also used as bridges! This might seem like an obvious idea today. But when people first came up with them it totally changed the way that they thought about irrigation and transportation.

All of these inventions were very important to future designs of dams and levees. But the most important thing about the Roman dams was that they were built to last. The Subiaco Dam was the tallest one that the ancient Romans built. It was 160 feet (49 m) high, making it the tallest dam in the world. It remained the tallest dam in the world until it was destroyed in the year 1305. That's

The town of Subiaco sits in the hills of Italy.
The Romans built one of their tallest dams here.

over a thousand years after it was built, and even then, it didn't fall apart on its own. It was actually destroyed by accident! Two monks decided to remove some layers of rocks from the dam in order to let more water through for irrigation. This weakened the structure. The next time that the river flooded, the dam burst. Who knows, maybe if those monks had left that dam alone, we could still go visit it today!

Chapter 2

IMPROVING DAMS AND LEVEES WITH TECHNOLOGY

Dams and levees have come a long way over the past five thousand years. They still keep water from flooding towns and help farmers water their crops. They also do much more. Over the years, engineers and scientists have come up with lots of inventions that changed the way we think about these structures.

Dams Generate Clean, Renewable Energy

Electricity is very important. Many dams use the power of water (hydropower) to make electricity that can be used in nearby communities. In fact, more than one-fifth of the electricity in the whole world comes from hydropower. That means that if you live near a body of water, the electricity that you use at home could well come from a dam!

Dams create hydropower using a water turbine. This is a big wheel with paddles on one end, a long shaft in the middle, and a generator on the other end. The water that flows through the dam runs over the big wheel. This makes the shaft spin. The generator gathers the energy made by the spinning shaft. Then it turns it into

The Daniel-Johnson Dam sits on the Manicouagan River. It was built in order to create hydroelectric power.

The Itaipu Dam

One of the most amazing dams on earth is the Itaipu Dam. It lies on the border of Brazil and Paraguay. It creates more hydropower than any other dam in the world. It supplies about 86 percent of the electricity used in Paraguay. The dam actually makes much more electricity than the people of Paraguay use every year. If they didn't share it with Brazil, it could power their entire country all by itself! Nearly all of the rest of Paraguay's electricity comes from two other dams. This makes it one of the only countries on earth that uses 100 percent renewable energy.

electricity, which is then sent to nearby power plants. These power plants are connected to the power grid. Water is always flowing through these types of dams. So this is a very good way to make electricity without a lot of work.

The best part about hydropower is that it is a form of renewable energy. Most types of energy come from resources that we will run out of one day. Coal, oil, and natural gas are forms of nonrenewable energy. If people only used resources like these to generate power, eventually there would be none left. We wouldn't be able to use electricity anymore. Thankfully, we also have renewable energy. This comes from resources that replenish themselves, like the sun, wind, and water. People will be able to use water to make electricity long after there is no oil or coal left on the entire planet. Right now, hydropower makes up more than

The Itaipu Dam in Brazil supplies the majority of Paraguay's electricity.

half of the world's renewable energy. Most of this comes from dams. Hopefully in the future, all of the energy that we use will be renewable.

Another great thing about renewable energy is that it is a very clean way to make electricity. We make electricity from coal and other fossil fuels by burning it and capturing the heat. When we do that, we release all kinds of nasty chemicals into the air. This is a major form of pollution, and it is bad for the planet. It also causes many different illnesses in people, like asthma and emphysema. Renewable energy doesn't have any of these harmful effects. If we start to use more of it, we'll help to heal the earth and make people live longer, healthier lives.

Modern Machines for Building Dams and Levees

In ancient times, workers used simple tools to build dams and levees. This was very difficult. It took a very long time. Sometimes, almost everyone in a town would help to build the structures little by little. They carried materials and dropped them into the water

A sheepsfoot roller helps the dam builder pack down the ground under the structure.

until they formed a barrier. Even after all of that hard work, most early dams and levees were destroyed as soon as a serious flood happened. Then local workers would have to start building them all over again.

Just like in the past, building a dam or levee today means moving huge amounts of earth. But workers don't need to do this by hand anymore. Instead, they use machines to remove, pack down, and fill in large amounts of rocks and soil. They do this much more quickly and use fewer workers.

Construction teams working on dams and levees use lots of heavy machinery. They might use dump trucks, backhoes, cranes, and bulldozers. They can also use power tools and explosives to make their work easier. You might be familiar with a lot of these machines since they are used in lots of different types of building. But there are lots of cool machines and attachments that are especially useful for making dams and levees.

One tool that is often used by dam and levee builders is a clamshell bucket. A clamshell bucket is a huge two-sided bucket. It has interlocking teeth on the bottom, which workers can attach to a crane. When it is lowered into the ground, the two sides split apart. When the crane operator lifts the bucket back up into the air, the sides come back together. This traps tons of dirt and rocks that can be dropped away from the place that is being dug up. It's like a gigantic version of the crane game that you can play at arcades!

It's very important for the ground under a dam or levee to be packed down and leveled perfectly. If this does not happen, the structure could weaken and break over time. Workers use a special machine to make sure that this step is done right the first time. It is called the sheepsfoot roller. A sheepsfoot roller is a lot like the steamrollers that are used to repave roads. But instead of being perfectly smooth, the roller is covered with lots of bumps that are shaped like hooves. When it rolls over soil, these bumps apply even pressure to the ground. This packs it much better than a regular steamroller would.

So far we've learned all about the ways that we've improved dams and levees over the centuries. Now let's find out more about the most important part of any infrastructure project: the workers!

Chapter 3

WHO BUILDS DAMS AND LEVEES?

These days it is easier than ever to build dams and levees. Still, building and maintaining them are huge projects. Many different types of workers are needed. In fact, governments have chosen to build more dams and levees during hard times so that more people can make a living. This happened a lot during the Great Depression. Let's take a look at some of the different types of jobs that are necessary to build and repair dams and levees.

Jobs Building Dams and Levees

Most of the workers involved in creating dams and levees are engineers. An engineer is a person who designs, builds, or maintains machines and infrastructure. First, a location for a dam or

Civil engineers look over plans for a new dam. They are in charge of overseeing the dam's design and construction.

levee is chosen. Then many different engineers get to work. They design the structure, make sure that it is safe to build, and oversee its actual construction.

Civil engineers decide which type of structure is best to use. They weigh the pros and cons of different designs. Then they draw up plans that the workers will follow. These engineers focus on how the structure will be built. Then they meet with other types of engineers who are experts in different areas of construction.

One expert in building dams and levees is a geotechnical engineer. These engineers check the ground beneath the work site. They let the civil engineers know if the ground is strong enough to hold the structure that they've designed. Civil engineers will also talk to engineering geologists and hydrologists. These are experts in figuring out exactly how strong the structure needs to be. It has to be able to hold back the water at the job site without bursting.

Mechanical engineers are another important part of the engineering team. They design the pipework, valves, and floodgates that need to be built into the structures. This is a very different job than designing the walls of the dam or levee itself.

Before construction can begin, one more type of engineer needs to get involved: the environmental engineer. This expert looks at how the construction project affects the environment. A lot of dams and levees are built near freshwater that people drink. This means that it's very important that they are built in a way that does not create too much pollution. These engineers will carefully go over all of the plans and make sure that the project isn't going to harm the local area. Once they have given the thumbs up, construction is ready to begin!

Engineers oversee every part of the construction process. Still, most of the people that actually build the structures are construction workers and laborers. These workers know how to

Safety Check

The work never stops on a dam, even after the engineers and workers are finished building it. Every state in America has a team of dam safety inspectors. Their job is to visit every dam in the area from time to time. They perform lots of different tests on the dams, making sure that they don't need any repairs. This is a very important job. It helps keep dams from failing and destroying nearby towns.

operate the different types of machinery. They are also great at working as a team and staying organized. They make sure that every part of the engineers's plans is being followed.

Workers dig tunnels to move water away from the job site. They must make sure that the ground is dry enough to build on. Then they dig out huge amounts of earth. They flatten it perfectly with sheepsfoot rollers and other machines. Then they lay the foundation (base) of the structure. They do this with concrete or other strong materials. The dam or levee is built on top of the foundation. Workers always make sure to double-check at every step that they are building everything correctly. Different teams specialize in building the different parts of the structures. Before long, a new dam or levee is ready!

Fewer Workers Needed

As you can see, there are still many jobs involved in building and maintaining dams and levees. But some jobs are no longer needed because of today's technology.

In ancient times, whole towns would work together to build dams and levees. They had to move water and huge amounts of dirt and rocks by hand or with basic tools. During the Industrial Revolution, many machines were invented to make these tasks

Environmental engineers must make sure that a dam or levee does not harm the environment.

Dam safety inspectors check the dam regularly to make sure there are no problems or flaws.

easier. That meant that a smaller group of people could complete even bigger projects.

Even though it got easier to build dams and levees, lots of workers were still needed not too long ago. When Hoover Dam was built in the early 1930s, more than twenty thousand men worked on the project. Most of them were simple laborers. Their job was to remove material from the work site, flatten the ground, and build up the dam piece by piece. These workers were paid almost nothing for hard, dangerous work. Many of them died in construction accidents.

Today, most people who work on dams and levees are experts of some kind. Many of them are engineers. Heavy machinery has replaced much of the hard labor. This means that dams and levees don't create as many jobs as they used to. But it also means that building them is much safer, more efficient, and more affordable. Before long, almost all of these construction jobs will be done by machines. Who knows, maybe someday robots will design and build entire dams and levees from start to finish!

Chapter 4

AMERICA'S GREATEST DAMS AND LEVEES

You've seen how dams and levees were built throughout history. You've learned about the different jobs that are involved in their design and construction. Now let's take a closer look at some of the most amazing dams and levees in America. They have changed the country and made life easier for millions of people.

Hoover Dam

Perhaps the most amazing dam in the United States is one that we already read about earlier in the book: Hoover Dam. It is located on the Colorado River, on the border between Nevada and Arizona. It is a huge gravity-arch dam made out of concrete. Hoover Dam is over 725 feet (220 m) tall, 1,244 feet (380 m) long,

Hoover Dam is probably the most famous dam in the United States.

Men work in the Black Canyon during the construction of the Boulder Dam. It was later renamed Hoover Dam.

and 45 feet (14 m) wide! It took five years to build. Construction started in 1931 and was finished in 1936. The dam cost $639 million in today's money. At the time, it was the largest concrete structure ever built.

Building Hoover Dam was very dangerous. By the time it was finished, 112 workers had died in accidents. Even more workers were hurt. At the time, many of the safety devices that construction workers now use hadn't been invented yet. Also, a lot of the most dangerous jobs that are now done by machines still had to be done by hand. Workers had fewer rights, especially the immigrant laborers who got the most dangerous tasks. Many people were willing to risk their lives to complete this project because there were so few jobs available in the country at the time.

To this day, Hoover Dam serves two main purposes for nearby states. First, it stores fresh water in Lake Mead. This is a very large reservoir that provides much of the drinking water for Las Vegas and other cities. Second, the dam makes a lot of electricity for Nevada, Arizona, and Southern California. Both of these roles are very important. The area around the dam is mostly desert, and many towns and cities wouldn't be able to exist without it. Unfortunately, the area has had years of constant drought. This means that Lake Mead is holding less water today than it ever has before. It also means that the water turbines in the dam are not able to make as much electricity. Engineers in the area are working

Looking for Work at Hoover Dam

Over five years, more than twenty thousand workers helped to build Hoover Dam. You will remember that the dam was designed to help create jobs during the Great Depression of the 1930s. At any one time, there could be three thousand to more than five thousand workers on the job. That may seem like a lot. But when Hoover Dam was announced, unemployed people from all over the country came to try to get a job working on it. Between ten and twenty thousand out-of-work laborers moved to the area during this time. Most of them ended up living in camps around the work site, hoping that a job would open up for them.

around the clock to update the dam. They want to make sure that it continues to work for many generations to come.

The Mississippi Levee System

One of the largest levee systems in the entire world is right here in America! A huge network of levees borders both sides of the Mississippi River. The levees were built to help stop the flooding that often happened along the river. The whole system is made up of more than 3,500 miles (5,632 kilometers) of levees. It starts in Missouri and follows the river all the way down to the Mississippi Delta in between Mississippi, Louisiana, and Arkansas.

French settlers were the first people to build levees along the Mississippi River. In the 1700s, they built 50 miles (80 km) of levees along the river. The levees were three 3 feet (1 m) high. The French built the levees in order to keep the city of New Orleans (now part of Louisiana) from flooding when the waters rose. About one hundred years later, the United States had bought all of the surrounding land from France. The American government knew that it had to improve the levee system. Starting in 1822, levees were built all along the river. They went as far north as Illinois.

Bit by bit, engineers have been improving the Mississippi levee system ever since. It took until the 1980s for it to stretch as far as it does today. By then the levees were an average of 24 feet (7.3 m) tall. Some of the tallest levees in the system are as high as 50 feet (15 m) tall! The system also has some of the longest individual levees on earth. This includes a single levee that is more than 375 miles (603 km) long. These levees have an important role, and when they fail, tragedy can strike. We'll learn all about what happened to the levees in New Orleans, Louisiana, in the next chapter.

Glen Canyon Dam

The last important American structure that we'll discuss in this chapter is Glen Canyon Dam. Like Hoover Dam, it is a concrete arch-gravity dam built on the Colorado River. But this one is located farther north, above the Grand Canyon. It was built between 1956 and 1966, and it created Lake Powell. This is one of the largest

Glen Canyon Dam. Notice the four tubes in the lower
right corner. They are releasing water from the reservoir
because of a water shortage in the area.

man-made reservoirs in the United States. It can hold up to 27.2 million acre-feet (32.3 million cubic meters) of water!

Glen Canyon Dam helps to make sure that the area has plenty of drinking water, even during long droughts. It also makes a huge amount of electricity. It is the second largest hydropower producer in the region (Hoover Dam is the first).

The dam does a lot of good for the community. But it has also caused controversy over the years. Glen Canyon was a beautiful and unique canyon that many people enjoyed for years. The canyon could no longer be enjoyed once it was flooded and turned into Lake Powell. Many environmental groups were upset with the decision to create the dam. They have been asking to have the dam removed ever since it was built.

Glen Canyon Dam has also had a major effect on the behavior of the Colorado River. The water is much calmer than it once was. It also doesn't reach the peak water levels that it did before the dam was built. This has been a disaster for several types of animals and plants that are native to the area, especially within the Grand Canyon. On top of all of this, every year a huge amount of water evaporates from Lake Powell before humans are able to use it.

Glen Canyon Dam is an example of the negative effect that dams and levees can have on the environment if they aren't properly planned, designed, and built. Today, environmental engineers work very hard to make sure that these mistakes are not repeated.

Chapter 5

WHEN DAMS AND LEVEES FAIL

We have learned a lot about how much good dams and levees can do for people. They store drinking water and make electricity. They also keep rivers and streams from flooding nearby areas. These structures can help make life easier when they are working correctly. But if they fail, the effects can be a disaster.

In this final chapter, we will look at two tragedies that happened when dams and levees failed in the United States. These sad tales show the importance of proper construction, inspections, and maintenance. They will also remind us that we must always be prepared for the worst.

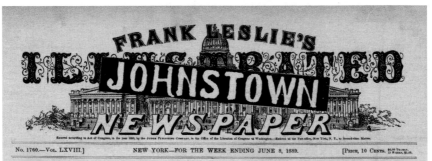

A New York newspaper features a drawing of deadly flooding in Johnstown, Pennsylvania, in 1889.

The Johnstown Flood of 1889

The South Fork Dam was built above the town of Johnstown, Pennsylvania, between 1838 and 1853. The dam created the reservoir of Lake Conemaugh. The lake supplied water to a major canal system that crossed the entire state. But the growing number of railroads meant that canals were no longer used. The dam and lake were abandoned and sold to the Pennsylvania Railroad.

Years later, a group bought the dam and lake from the railroad. They turned it into a luxury resort community. They made many changes to the dam that weakened it and caused it to spring leaks. The developers patched the leaks with mud and straw. They did not make the proper repairs to ensure that the South Fork Dam was safe.

On May 31, 1889, the area was hit with the biggest storm that was ever recorded there. In less than a day, 6 to 10 inches (15–25 centimeters) of rain fell. The water level of the lake rose so high that it was almost coming over the dam. Workers did their best to try to repair the dam and keep it from breaking. But it was too late. The dam burst and sent 3.8 billion gallons (14.3 billion liters) of water rushing downstream toward Johnstown.

First, the water ripped through several small towns between the dam and Johnstown. It killed almost four hundred people. It swept heavy debris like houses and train cars farther downstream. By the time the water hit Johnstown, there was already almost 10 feet

A man sits on a tree that has gotten stuck in an overturned house after the Johnstown Flood.

(3 m) of floodwater from the rain. The people of the town were trapped. The rushing water devastated the town. It killed thousands of people and destroyed sixteen hundred homes. In the end, the Johnstown Flood killed 2,208 people and caused almost $500 million in damages. At the time, it was the largest loss of civilian life in United States history.

This tragic story shows how important it is to make sure that dams are built properly and safely. The people who bought the South Fork Dam didn't take care of it, and many people paid the price for their mistakes. But every tragic story has a silver lining. After the flood, a new disaster relief group came into the area to help clean up. It was the American Red Cross. The group brought in a team of fifty doctors and nurses. They were led by their founder, Clara Barton. The team stayed for five months. This was one of the very first times that the American Red Cross helped after a disaster. It showed the world that people could band together and help each other during hard times. People from all over donated millions of dollars to help the town.

Hurricane Katrina

The next example of dams and levees failing happened much more recently than the Johnstown Flood. Hurricane Katrina was a huge tropical cyclone. It made landfall in southeastern Louisiana as a Category 3 hurricane on August 29, 2005. The storm caused major

Clara Barton

Clara Barton is an amazing figure in United States history. She was one of the most important nurses for the Union army during the Civil War. She was a major force in the fight to end slavery. She helped to get women the right to vote. And she was the founder of the American Red Cross, which still operates today. Barton lived at a time when women had almost no power. She did not let this stop her. Clara Barton proved that women could overcome major obstacles and make the world a better place.

Workers repair a canal levee in New Orleans after Hurricane Katrina.

flooding all along the Gulf of Mexico, from Florida to Texas. But the most damage occurred in the city of New Orleans, Louisiana.

New Orleans is located in the Mississippi Delta. This is an area where the Mississippi River empties into the Gulf of Mexico. The city is only a few miles inland from the gulf. It is also completely surrounded by the Mississippi River and two lakes. Normally, it is protected from flooding by the levees and floodwalls that we learned about in the previous chapter. But Hurricane Katrina was just too powerful. The levees and floodwalls failed in fifty different places. Eighty percent of the city was flooded with as much as 15 feet (4.5 m) of water.

The whole world watched in horror as New Orleans was destroyed. Most of the city's residents were able to evacuate, but almost fifteen hundred people lost their lives. The storm caused $70 billion in property damage. Government groups responded to the disaster, but it took a very long time for help to arrive. Many people did not think the government reacted quickly enough. Since then, there have been many changes to the way that the government prepares for emergencies. They want to make sure that they do a much better job in the future.

The government's slow response to Hurricane Katrina was only one part of the problem. The disaster never would have happened in the first place if the levees and floodwalls around the city had been built correctly. It took engineers a long time to investigate what happened. Finally they announced that the levees were big enough to keep the floodwaters at bay, but there was a major flaw in their design and construction. In order to save money, the metal pilings that make up the backbone of the levees were driven only 17 feet (5 m) into the ground. They were supposed to be buried at least 31 feet (9.4 m) deep. This mistake caused a great deal of death and destruction. It also reminded engineers everywhere how important it is to build infrastructure safely and correctly.

Since the hurricane, nearly all of the levees around New Orleans have been rebuilt. Engineers have brought these structures up to code, and they are stronger than ever. Now that these improvements are in place, the city is protected from flooding once again. Hopefully, Hurricane Katrina will be the last disaster to ever strike New Orleans. If so, it will be because of the hard work of engineers and the life-saving abilities of one of our favorite structures: levees.

CHRONOLOGY

3000 BCE The first dams and levees are built in Mesopotamia.

150 BCE Ancient Romans invent concrete.

60 CE Ancient Romans build the Subiaco Dam, the world's tallest dam at the time.

200 Kallanai Dam is built in India.

1760 Industrial Revolution begins, changing the way that people build dams and levees.

1849 Modern water turbine is invented.

1878 World's first hydroelectric system is built.

1889 Johnstown Flood occurs, causing the most civilian deaths in American history.

1931 Construction begins on Hoover Dam.

2005 Storm surges from Hurricane Katrina cause the New Orleans levees to fail, flooding the city.

2016 Itaipu Dam breaks a world record for generating hydroelectricity.

WORDS TO KNOW

arch dam A dam that is curved upstream to make its walls even stronger.

buttress A projecting support of stone or brick built against a wall.

buttress dam A dam that is reinforced by a series of support pillars.

dam A barrier that stops or restricts the flow of water or underground streams.

drought A long period of very dry weather.

embankment dam A dam made of many layers of compacted rocks and soil.

engineer A person who designs, builds, or maintains machines, engines, or public works.

gravity dam A vertical dam built to be heavy enough to keep water from bursting it.

hydropower Power that comes from the energy of moving water.

irrigation Supplying water to land or crops to help growth.

levee A long ridge or wall that regulates water levels.

renewable energy Energy from a source that does not run out when it is used.

reservoir A manmade lake where water is collected to be used.

water turbine A machine that changes the energy of moving water into electricity.

LEARN MORE

Books

Gabriel, Luke. *The Hoover Dam*. Mankato, MN: The Children's World, 2014.

Latham, Donna. *Canals and Dams: Investigate Feats of Engineering with 25 Projects*. White River Junction, VT: Nomad Press, 2013.

Loh-Hagan, Virginia. *Dams*. Ann Arbor, MI: Cherry Lake, 2017.

Pettiford, Rebecca. *Dams.* Minneapolis, MN: Jump!, 2016.

Websites

Build a Dam

pbskids.org/zoom/activities/sci/buildadam.html

With a few common materials, you can build your own dam!

Hoover Dam Facts for Kids Video

easyscienceforkids.com/hoover-dam-facts-for-kids-video

View an interesting video about the history and construction of Hoover Dam.

INDEX